LOUISA May ALCOTT

A Life from Beginning to End

Copyright © 2020 by Hourly History.

Table of Contents

Introduction

Louisa May Alcott was born in Pennsylvania on November 29, 1832, but her family soon moved to Massachusetts, the center of the nineteenth-century transcendental movement. Transcendentalists Henry David Thoreau and Ralph Waldo Emerson were to be lifelong friends and neighbors.

Louisa's parents, Bronson and Abigail, were fervent abolitionists and advocates of women's rights, and when Louisa was 15, the Alcotts worked with the Underground Railroad, helping escaped slaves move north. Bronson, a teacher, was frequently out of work due to his progressive beliefs, such as accepting a black student into his school, and Louisa soon became responsible for helping to support her parents and three sisters. Because of her father's sometimes irresponsible zealotry, Louisa learned early on to rely on herself and made a vow never to marry.

Teaching was one respectable way for a young lady of her time to earn money. Being a writer was another. Louisa began her career as an author with rather lurid and daring short stories which she published under a nom de plume. When her publisher insisted she try writing a children's novel, Louisa reluctantly put aside her fiery short stories and wrote *Little Women*, the novel for which she became best known. It was a tremendous success and is still enjoyed by people around the world. Thanks to *Little Women* and its sequels, *Little Men* and *Jo's Boys,* Louisa was able to help her family financially throughout their lives.

As an early feminist, being independent was crucial to Louisa. She worked as a nurse during the American Civil War and fought for women's right to vote, becoming the first woman in Concord to register to vote. Louisa May Alcott never set out to be a writer; she became one out of necessity to support her family. Nevertheless, she managed to write one of the most memorable and enduring children's books ever, which is still being read 150 years after its publication.

Chapter One

The Alcott Family

"Peddling is a hard place to serve God, but a capital one to serve Mammon."

—Amos Bronson Alcott

Louisa's life was heavily influenced by her parents. Her father Amos Bronson Alcott, born in 1799, realized early on that he wanted to become a teacher. Before managing to find work as an educator, he eked out a living as a peddler of goods by going door to door. His own lack of formal education made him realize the important role education played in people's lives. His views on teaching the young were contradictory to the prevailing beliefs of the times, however, and Bronson frequently found himself out of work.

Bronson believed that the content of early education had the power to form a person for life, a concept that is accepted in modern times but was not understood in the nineteenth century. He also insisted that the young should enjoy learning and attempted to turn his lessons into a pleasant experience. This did not sit well with many of the Calvinist parents of his students, who believed that man was born sinful, punishment was man's natural fate, and only corporal punishment could banish the sin out of children. In other words, children needed to be spanked to be kept in line. Bronson would eventually test his theories on his own children and included art, music, dance, and other subjects in their general education.

When Bronson took a job as a teacher in Cheshire, Connecticut during the mid-1820s, his controversial methods soon attracted attention from fellow social reformer Samuel Joseph May. Like Bronson, Samuel was a fervent advocate of education, women's rights, and the abolition of slavery, and the two became fast friends.

When Samuel introduced Bronson to his sister, Abigail, she called Bronson's style of education "very attractive" and found him to be "an intelligent, philosophic, modest man." But although Abigail was quickly smitten with Bronson, they were awkward around each other. Bronson refused to pursue Abigail until he was certain he would not be rejected, and after one of their meetings, Abigail wrote in her diary that his "reserve chilled me into silence." It would take two years from their first meeting for them to work up the nerve for a kiss.

Bronson's hesitant attitude caused Abigail tremendous dismay, and she constantly wondered if she was good enough for him and how she could improve. This flawed nineteenth-century belief—that women had to earn the approval of men, but not the other way around—would eventually trickle down to Louisa and become a significant theme in her writing.

Although Bronson was progressive for his time, he still held the notion that women were meant to subjugate their desires to the desires of their men—a fact which became apparent when Abigail's sister died. Abigail was understandably devasted, but Bronson wrote in his diary that "I have led her thought regarding herself to regarding me." In other words, despite her grief, her attention needed to be on him. Bronson firmly believed that his advice would make her a better person. When Abigail escaped to her brother's house for solace, Bronson wrote to her about his theories on women. Women, he explained, were responsible for the moral compass of a household. Men were responsible for the intellectual mood.

Louis Godey, a contemporary publisher on social rules and marital advice, wrote, "Be to her faults a little blind; be to her virtues very kind; let all her ways be unconfined; and place your padlock on her mind." This liberal advice to treat one's wife kindly also advised men to not let their wives think for themselves. Bronson's daughters, especially Louisa, were to struggle with that concept later in life. These dynamics, which were the norm for the times, would eventually find their way into Louisa's *Little Women*.

Finally, Abigail took the initiative in the relationship. She went to Boston to recommend Bronson for a number of teaching positions. When he finally opened another school, Abigail insinuated herself into his new life by continuously helping him with day to day activities. She remained a constant presence. At last, in May of 1830, the two were married.

Boston was an exciting place to be. It was a beautiful city, with lovely mansions and the Commons, a public park available to all. The harbor was filled with activities with merchant boats arriving and leaving. Soon, however, Bronson's new school faltered again as parents refused to accept his radical teaching methods. The Alcott family relocated to Germantown, Philadelphia in late 1830, where

Bronson opened another innovative school. Abigail was by this point pregnant the couple's first child, a daughter named Anna. Louisa May Alcott, the second daughter, was then born one year later on November 29, 1832.

Anna, the first daughter, watched her father carefully for any signs of approval or disapproval. Even as a toddler, Anna understood that his love for her depended on his approval of her action. She learned quickly to behave in the proper manner and became his favorite child. Louisa, on the other hand, was more quick-tempered and frequently cried, which put her in second place for her father's affection. While Bronson never resorted to physical punishment, the withdrawal of his love and affection from his daughters may have been even more hurtful.

Bronson continuously made notes on the physical and spiritual development of his growing family. He wrote that Anna, his favorite, was blond like her father, while Louisa was darker like her mother. Light hair, he concluded, equaled a higher level of morality.

Chapter Two

The Transcendental Movement

"Far away there in the sunshine are my highest aspirations. I may not reach them, but I can look up and see their beauty, believe in them, and try to follow where they lead."

—Louisa May Alcott

Like in other schools in which he had taught, Bronson slowly lost his students in Germantown when parents became suspicious of his teaching methods. At first, the Alcotts sold off some of their belongings to help ends meet. Bronson firmly believed in the natural, God-given division between men and women, and it humiliated him that he was unable to provide for his family. He understood that if he were less rigid about his ideals, he could make a living. That, however, Bronson was unwilling to do. Principles came before pragmatic need, and his family needed to accept that.

Bronson begged the parents of his students to believe in his methods, but more and more parents placed their children elsewhere. Frustrated, the family returned to Boston and took rooms on Bedford Street. Elizabeth Peabody, an educator whose methods aligned with

Bronson's, found a few students for him from Boston's best families.

In September of 1834, Bronson opened the Temple School at the Masonic Temple in Boston, where a number of students were boarded. Half of his students were girls, and he expected them to be a positive moral influence on the other half. Miss Peabody assisted for a few hours a day. However, the more she saw Bronson in action, the less she began to think of him. For example, he would encourage his students to confess some wrongdoing. Upon doing so, he had the young offender hit him. Miss Peabody saw this form of penance as a way to force the child to feel guilty at whatever anger he might be feeling. Bronson also openly discussed birth to a class of both girls and boys. Such frankness horrified her. Any allusion to sex was unthinkable during these staid times. Miss Peabody left Temple School in 1836 rather than endure any more of Bronson's boldness.

In Boston during these years, the Unitarian Church was making some inroads into attracting followers. Contrary to the city's established Protestant churches, Unitarianism was a liberal and individualistic approach to religion. The transcendental movement then grew out of Unitarianism in 1836 when New England intellectuals such as Ralph Waldo Emerson founded the Transcendental Club. Thanks to his friendship with Emerson, Henry David Thoreau, and Margaret Fuller, Bronson developed a strong interest in transcendentalism and joined the club soon after its founding.

Transcendentalists believed that a person could improve his or her life through hard work. According to Emerson,

"It is one of the most beautiful compensations of this life that no man can sincerely try to help another without helping himself." For Bronson, this would have translated into pleasing others, except that he was more concerned about being pleased than pleasing. Much of Louisa's writing would later incorporate these beliefs, although she developed her own ideas on the subject. She was far more pragmatic than Bronson and was more concerned with what worked in daily life.

This transcendental group, which lauded the inherent goodness of all things, became an important part of Bronson's life, and in class, the subjects he taught were from this point on studied from a transcendental moral point of view. When transcendentalists noticed, they were quite encouraged and turned Bronson into a minor celebrity. After receiving this recognition, Bronson became even more convinced that his teaching methods were the way forward.

Bronson frequently brought his oldest daughter, Anna, to class to show her off as an example of the perfect little girl. Louisa, meanwhile, was left at home with her mother and new baby sister, Elizabeth. As the middle child, who wasn't her father's favorite and who didn't get the attention that the infant in the family did, Louisa's only recourse was to misbehave to receive any type of notice. Needless to say, her behavioral offenses only served to alienate her father even more. Elizabeth Peabody, who was often with the children, was concerned about some of Louisa's violent tantrums.

Bronson felt the education of his children was too important to relegate solely to their mother, Abigail. He was especially concerned that Louisa, if left unchecked, would negatively influence the much more submissive Anna. After he spent a week with them, he was pleased to see how obedient and well-behaved Anna was. She often greeted Bronson with, "Father, I love you for punishing me." Louisa, on the other hand, controlled her temper merely out of fear, not from a personal desire to please.

Bronson continually put his two eldest daughters to the test to see who would obey him out of a desire to please him. Pleasing him had to be their number one goal. Anna invariably came out of ahead. The rebellious Louisa simply couldn't live up to her father's expectations. To make matters worse, when she turned to her mother, Louisa frequently found Abigail too overwhelmed with her own duties to pay much attention to her daughter. While Abigail struggled to take care of the household, she received a letter from her father telling her how she had disappointed him by marrying a man who kept losing his job and couldn't provide for his family. Abigail was torn between the men in her life.

In late 1836, Bronson published a treatise on education, *Conversations with Children on the Gospels.* In this book, he questioned whether miracles were real and whether everyone wasn't a part of God. To make things worse, he even questioned the Virgin birth. The book was not well-received. Bronson was seen by most as either insane or ignorant. The *Boston Courier* declared that "*Conversations* was a more indecent and obscene book (we can say nothing of its absurdity) than any other we ever saw exposed for sale."

Again, parents started pulling their children from Bronson's school. The entire family had to move to a smaller, less expensive space in Boston's South End. Money became very tight. They couldn't afford tea or coffee, and they mostly subsided on cheap vegetables. Abigail had to make do without any household help, and her health took a turn for the worse. She suffered through a premature birth of the couple's fourth child, a stillborn son. While all this was happening, Abigail hoped for a reconciliation with her father. The old man had a hard time accepting the notoriety she had to endure thanks to her husband, but he did agree to come for occasional visits.

With Abigail ill, Bronson and the girls took over many household duties. Bronson began to implement the suggestions of radical nutritionist Sylvester Graham and eliminated meat and dairy entirely from the family's diet, making the family vegan before the term was coined. Abigail and the girls frequently pleaded for a bit of meat but to no avail.

Bronson referred to his daughters as the "living manifestation of my intellect." Clearly, he saw them as reflections of himself rather than individual people. Anna, still his favorite and always eager for improvement, worked hard around the apartment. For her eighth birthday, Bronson gave her a copy of *Pilgrim's Progress* with encouragement that she should continue her self-improvements. This, of course, left Louisa wondering if she'd ever become good enough. One day, when Anna and Louisa went romping on the Commons, Anna reported back to their father that Louisa had gotten her shoes wet. It was as if love were finite in this family, with the children each out for a larger slice of the pie.

As much as she longed for her father's love, Louisa refused to conform and remained her rebellious self. When she was six, she ran away and strolled through the streets of Boston. Eventually, she fell asleep in a doorway. When she was finally found and returned home, Abigail tied her to the sofa, knowing that this loss of freedom would be harder for Louisa to bear than the fact that she had failed to please her father. Mostly, she'd already given up on that.

Chapter Three

Fruitlands, the Utopian Dream

"The band of brothers began by spading garden and field;
but a few days of it lessened their ardor amazingly."

—Louisa May Alcott

Boston was undergoing some exciting changes during the early 1800s. No subject was more prevalent than slavery, and Massachusetts was the first state to pass antislavery laws in the country. Boston was the home of the Adams family, all of whom had worked diligently in opposition to slavery, especially John Adams and John Quincy Adams. Boston's freedom-loving heritage was alive and well.

Decades before the American Civil War, the city was at the epicenter of an abolitionist movement. In 1783, Chief Justice William Cushing declared that in Massachusetts, there could be "no such thing as perpetual servitude of a rational Creature." In other words, the selling of human beings was forbidden.

Both Bronson and Abigail were staunch abolitionists and instilled this belief into their children. According to Louisa, she "became an abolitionist at a very early age." Bronson then went a step further in 1839 by admitting an African American student to his school. This immediately sparked protests among the parents of his other students, and before long, almost all of his pupils had left, forcing him to close the school.

After the failure of the Temple School, the Alcott family moved to Concord, which put them amid the leading minds of the times. Ralph Waldo Emerson, Henry David Thoreau, Nathaniel Hawthorne, Horace Mann, among others, called this charming New England town their home. Bronson built a vegetable garden, which was the family's main source of food. He hired himself out to chop wood, but there was little call for his services. They all-too-often went hungry, and whenever Louisa acted out, she was sent to her room without supper.

Apart from that, she loved Concord. The rural location gave her the opportunity to run and play and burn off much of her energy. She followed Henry Thoreau on his daily walks, and she and her sister Anna eventually attended the Concord Academy, which was run by Henry's brother, John. Henry taught there, as well. Unfortunately, John Thoreau died in 1842.

When Abigail had her fourth daughter, also named Abigail May but eventually called May, Anna took over many of the duties of caring for the new baby in her continuous efforts to please Bronson. Louisa much preferred doing the dishes, which rated lower in the good deeds department in Bronson's opinion. As had become the natural order of things in this family, Anna remained closer to her father while Louisa was close to her mother.

In 1842, Bronson learned that two British reformers had opened an Alcott School in England, which was being run according to his teaching principles. Emerson offered to pay for Bronson to visit the school. Bronson was pleased with what he saw in London and approved of the school. The founders of the school had added their own twists to Bronson's teachings, such as celibacy. Apart from the Alcott School, Bronson disliked everything about England. Drinkers of beer and eaters of meat revolted him.

Abigail missed her husband terribly after he left, but soon, she seemed to appreciate the calm brought by his absence. She found it a lot easier to expound on his virtues when he wasn't around. Louisa positively thrived in her father's absence. She went exploring and enjoyed discovering new things, and she also tried to behave for her mother's sake. Seeing Abigail overwhelmed with family duties and the new infant, Louisa started to take on more responsibilities around the house. It pleased her to be able to be of help to her mother.

When Bronson was expected to return, Abigail and the girls cleaned the house from top to bottom to make him feel welcome. His trip to London had greatly enhanced his self-assurance. Being loved was no longer enough. Now, he expected to be revered. He was, after all, a well-known educator.

The fact that Abigail remained in the marriage can easily be explained by the fact that divorce was almost unthinkable at the time. She also seems to have genuinely loved Bronson despite his shortcomings. When he decided to practice celibacy, she pretended agreement. Now that Bronson was back, Abigail also had to go back to feeding her family only vegetables. This soon began to affect her already fragile health.

Louisa could see the strain between her parents, even if she was too young to understand the cause. The high spirits that had marked his absence now turn into the sullen rebellion that she'd always shown. Since Henry Thoreau was now spending his time with Bronson instead of her, she'd lost a valued friend as well.

The inability to support his family took its toll on Bronson. Their poverty was a great humiliation for the family, but no school in Concord would let him teach. Still, he never failed to lecture his family on how to they could improve themselves.

While Louisa went through the travails of adolescence, she looked on as her mother suffered and struggled. Was this what women were supposed to endure? The only advice Abigail gave on the topic of relationships was to avoid boys at all costs. One major goal solidified in Louisa's mind: as long as she lived, she would never be dependent on a man.

In 1843, Bronson, with the financial support of fellow transcendentalist Charles Lane, established a commune called Fruitlands on a farm in Harvard, Massachusetts. Fruitlands was meant to be an incarnation of transcendentalist principles and Bronson's educational theories. Its members were only permitted fruits and vegetables as sustenance and tilled the land without the use of animal labor.

While Bronson traveled to raise money for his utopia, Abigail was left to do the backbreaking work. Ideals and reality once again conflicted. Fruitlands had to be abandoned in less than a year. Louisa, once again a witness to Bronson's idealistic failures, would later try to correct those failures in her books. She grew up immersed in transcendentalist ideals and would embrace them always, even if somewhat differently than Bronson. Her later novels, especially *An Old-Fashioned Girl* and *Little Women,* were intended to turn transcendentalism into a workable philosophy for children.

After Fruitlands, Bronson moved his family back to Concord to be close to Emerson's house. Emerson deeply admired Bronson's self-assurance and unwavering conviction. He could speak on any topic with confidence and poise, something Emerson wasn't able to do. What some people would consider rudeness, Bronson deemed honesty. Emerson and Bronson would remain life-long friends, and Emerson would financially support Bronson and the Alcotts during many of those years.

Abigail, like her husband, was a social reformer. She believed in—and advocated to her daughters—women's right to vote. After the disaster at Fruitlands, however, she became much less idealistic and far more pragmatic, which Louisa picked up. What good was a pure ideology if it didn't work? From his progressive schools to the Fruitlands experiment, all of Bronson's idealistic attempts had failed miserably. As Abigail put it, "Give me one day of practical philosophy; it is worth a century of speculation and discussion." This was a lesson that Louisa learned at a young age and embraced.

Chapter Four

Working to Support the Family

"Some people seemed to get all sunshine, and some all shadow."

—Louisa May Alcott

When Abigail's father died, there was hope for some relief of the family's dire financial situation. Bronson, meanwhile, had decided that he should not be working for wages; instead, he'd travel and lecture on transcendentalism. In effect, he would never work to support his family again.

In the fall of 1844, Abigail's father's estate was settled. She ended up with $1,000, money that was badly needed. Emerson loaned her an additional $500. Finally, Abigail was able to look for a house. Bronson, who had declared himself against private ownership, had no part in that deal. On April 1, 1845, Abigail moved her family into their new home, which they called Hillside. Like their previous home, it was close to Emerson.

While Abigail worried about finances, Bronson kept busy doing some gardening. Silently at his side, Louisa planted and weeded. While she enjoyed their time together, it bothered her that her father didn't do anything real for the family while her mother took on more and more work. By this point, Louisa and Anna had started attending the local school in Concord, while their father taught the two younger girls. Louisa's mood lightened considerably when she could spend time away from home, and she even began to write poetry.

At the age of 14, Louisa was becoming conscious of her sexuality, and it disturbed her. Bronson had withdrawn from any physical contact with what he considered his troubled daughter. Any type of kissing was banned in the Alcott family, and there was little or no hugging. Confused over something she couldn't discuss with anyone, Louisa internalized her normal teenage fantasies.

When Abigail arranged for Louisa to have her own room at Hillside, Louisa began to write thinly-veiled love letters to her friend, 43-year-old Emerson. Of course, she never sent them. She fantasized about him a lot, though. Undoubtedly, Emerson was never aware of her feelings toward him. Louisa had other fantasies as well, involving being happy, famous, and rich one day. She assumed that if she were famous and rich, she wouldn't feel as if something was wrong with her. She didn't want to become a self-sacrificing woman like Abigail. She'd seen her mother suffer for too many years. According to Abigail, God blessed men but forgot about women. Louisa thought she might be able to avoid this by becoming famous and rich. Certainly, the chaos Bronson caused throughout his life for the family did not make being a wife very appealing to Louisa.

At this point, Bronson was receiving money from Emerson while loudly denouncing anyone who worked for a living and declaring that he had earned to be supported by the community. In his journal, Emerson wrote that Bronson's "unpopularity is not at all wonderful."

Before the arrival of winter, the family had eaten all the contents of the vegetable garden, and no one in Concord would extend them any more credit. With Bronson assuming that fate would provide, Abigail had to take action. She rented out Hillside and moved the family back to Boston. There was some chance of her finding a job in a large city.

The move left Louisa miserable. Instead of romping through her beloved green countryside, she would be crammed into a tiny apartment. There would no longer be Emerson or Thoreau for conversation. She and her sisters, stuck in the city, began writing and putting on plays and skits in their tiny living quarters. The plays did a lot to make Louisa feel more content after losing Hillside. Taking on roles and pretending to be someone else helped her forget the misery she felt at having to live in Boston.

Bronson rented rooms above Elizabeth Peabody's bookstore on West Street. There, he could talk to his transcendentalist friends and lecture anyone who would listen. A group of like-minded men suggested forming a club and offered to pay the rent for Bronson's rooms. Nothing could have made him happier. Before leaving for his club each morning, he checked Anna and Louisa's diaries. They were not permitted any privacy. He praised Anna for her concern about other people and admonished Louisa for thinking selfish thoughts. With Abigail busy with charity work, the 17-year-old Louisa felt depressed, even suicidal. "So every day is a battle, and I'm so tired I don't want to live. Only, it's cowardly to die until you've done something."

Abigail earned money by distributing goods to the poor. She, Anna, and Louisa also taught three black children how to read and write. Abigail was appalled that Boston had no reasonable educational system for African Americans. After years of being made to feel inadequate by Bronson, Abigail was finally able to take pride in her accomplishments.

Friends and relatives began to comment on Bronson's refusal to work and support his family. Bronson became less and less popular. Finally, Abigail's uncle gave her his large house to live in, which at least gave the family more space. To supplement the family's income, it was decided that the two oldest girls, Anna and Louisa, had to find jobs. Anna began work as a governess in Lenox, Massachusetts. Louisa, meanwhile, ran a school in Boston's South End. From this point forward, both girls contributed to the family's financial situation.

Louisa continued to work diligently while worrying about her mother and sisters. She dreamed of buying a house for them to live in. The plan did not include Bronson.

Chapter Five

A Writer is Born

"I want to do something splendid . . . Something heroic or wonderful that won't be forgotten after I'm dead . . . I think I shall write books."

—Louisa May Alcott

Louisa had been dabbling in poetry for a few years without any real goals, but in 1851, her first poem was published in *Peterson's Magazine*, one of the most popular women's magazines at the time. Louisa was gratified at her accomplishment, and this revived her old fantasies about fame. Perhaps she could achieve prominence, after all. Abigail warned her she was too young to consider such plans.

The family finally moved to a nicer house when Nathaniel Hawthorne bought Hillside in 1852. Both Anna and Louisa were taking care of children and opened another school together to provide some income. "Father idle," was Louisa's sarcastic comment about the situation.

In an attempt to realize her fantasy about fame, Louisa brought some of her poetry to James Field, a publisher and owner of a bookstore on School Street. She wanted his opinion on her potential to make money off her writing. Field tried to be kind, but he firmly told her to stick with teaching. She had no aptitude for writing, he said. For

Louisa, who had been dreaming of a prosperous future that did not include poverty, it was a devasting blow. She had no wealthy husband to depend on. Now, apparently, she didn't even have writing talent. Louisa recovered remarkably quickly though. With her mother and sisters to look after, she couldn't afford to wallow in self-pity. Instead, she continued writing.

By 1854, Louisa's *The Rival Prima Donnas*, a romantic drama, and *Flower Fables*, a compilation of fairy tales, had been published. Louisa also wrote stories for the *SaturdayEvening Gazette*. The money helped a great deal. At the same time, Emerson set up a fund to help support the Alcotts. While Louisa was waiting to achieve fame and fortune, the family moved to Walpole, New Hampshire to save some money. In Walpole, they built another vegetable garden, which Bronson attended. Louisa joined the Amateur Dramatic Company and wrote plays which were performed by the four sisters. It was all fun, but there was no money coming in.

In desperation, Louisa moved back to Boston, where she continued to write and took up sewing. When she had any extra money, she sent clothes and fineries home to her sisters. Lizzie, as her younger sister Elizabeth was called, especially loved pretty outfits. Louisa knew her family was depending on her. To her father, she wrote pointedly, "though an Alcott, I can support myself."

A major worry for her by 1858 was the deteriorating health of her younger sister, 22-year-old Lizzie. The girl barely ate and couldn't get out of bed. It became obvious she didn't have long to live. Abigail and Louisa remained at her bedside until the end. With Lizzie dead and Anna soon to be married, Louisa saw the family she knew and loved disappear. Anna's marriage put Louisa in a strange position. She didn't want a husband, which to her implied dependence, something she had vowed never to be. Yet single women in the mid-nineteenth century faced constant rejection and grief because they lacked a husband.

In April of 1859, Louisa, Emerson, and Thoreau went to hear a speech by abolitionist John Brown. He spoke rousingly about conditions in Kansas and the need for help. He raised $2,000 that evening, which he would put to use a few months later at Harper's Ferry. Louisa was inspired by Brown's fervor. War was imminent and, with so much frustration eating away at her, Louisa hoped for war not for political reasons but as an outlet for her troubling anger within.

In the years leading up to the American Civil War, Louisa sold several stories to the prestigious *Atlantic Monthly*, which paid her very well. Still dreaming of fame, she began working on her first novel, *Moods*, which would eventually be published in 1864. The heroine, Sylvia Yule, is a moody tomboy based on Louisa herself. Wanting a bit of adventure in her life, Sylvia accompanies her brother and two of his friends on a trip. The two friends, based on Louisa's secret fantasies, Emerson and Thoreau, both fall in love with Sylvia. She chooses the wrong suitor and marries him. Ultimately, Sylvia renounces both the man she marries and the man she loves and returns to single life.

Louisa herself kept her distance from eligible men, but approaching the age of 30, she still entertained her childhood fantasies. They clearly were safer than the real thing.

Chapter Six

Alcott during the American Civil War

"I believe that it is as much a right and duty for women to do something with their lives as for men and we are not going to be satisfied with such frivolous parts as you give us."

—Louisa May Alcott

On April 15, 1861, the shots fired at Fort Sumter rang in the bloodiest war America had ever experienced. In Boston, volunteers marched off, and Louisa May was among those remaining, wishing them God-speed.

Back in Concord, Abigail was ill again, and Louisa rushed home to take care of the household. The constant financial struggle continued to plague her. Her married sister Anna knew how much Louisa resented wearing rags and sent her a package of nice clothing. Louisa appreciated the gesture.

Meanwhile, Henry Thoreau became ill and started to fade more each day, just as Lizzie had done. He refused to acknowledge that anything was wrong. When asked if he was at peace with God, he answered, "I did not know that we had ever quarreled." Thoreau passed away on May 6, 1862. Emerson, always generous, arranged for the burial.

In between her household duties and her writing, Louisa sewed shirts and bandages for the Union Army. With the war escalating, women were called upon to be trained as nurses for the wounded by the supervisor of nurses, Dorothy Dix, in Washington. This was the type of adventure for which Louisa had longed, and it was for a cause she desperately believed in. She applied and was soon on her way for training in Washington.

Washington was nothing like the beautiful and refined Boston with which she was familiar. The city had no sewage system until 1863, and refuse and garbage was everywhere. Farm animals roamed the lawn at the White House and the streets. Many people, especially escaped slaves, were living in squalor. The water was unfit to drink, and rats and cockroaches were everywhere. Prostitutes and thieves were doing a thriving business. Corpses were left on the streets. More people were dying of typhus than of war wounds.

Nurses' training began at 6:00 am at the Union Hotel Hospital. The place was cold and dirty (Florence Nightingale's imperative for cleanliness still wasn't universally accepted). Louisa fed patients, cleaned wounds, and saw to their comfort and needs. After the Battle of Fredericksburg, the hospital was filled with more maimed and wounded than she could ever have imagined.

After three weeks, Louisa was diagnosed with typhus pneumonia. She became very ill and lost most of her hair. Bronson was notified and came to see her. Although Louisa resisted, it became clear she could no longer continue to work. Feeling as if she had failed again, she returned to Concord. Her health would never be as good as it had been, and she remained sickly for the rest of her life. It turned out that she'd acquired mercury poisoning from the medicine she had received for her typhus.

Back in Concord was where Louisa began writing her lurid, sensational stories for Boston newspapers. The first story was called *Pauline's Passions and Punishment,* for which she received the goodly sum of $100. These passionate stories about murders and other crimes came from the very core of Louisa, a part that she could never admit to. She wrote about smart women who are far from innocent. She loved writing them as they allowed for a type of emotional release young women of those times were not allowed to have. For five years, Louisa published the stories under the pen name of A. M. Barnard. Writing anonymously allowed Louisa to give free rein to her fantasies.

In *A Long Fatal Love Chase,* a disheartened young woman named Rosamond Vivian lives a lonely life with her grandfather. She states, "I often feel as if I'd gladly sell my soul to Satan for a year of freedom." Almost immediately, Rosamond encounters a man called Phillip Tempest. He is clearly bad news, but Rosamond, believing she can save him, marries him. Tempest whisks her away to a life of luxury in Nice, but Rosamond soon realizes just how cruel her husband can be. She had asked for the devil, and that was exactly who she has ended up with. It turns out Tempest already has a wife and child, making a mockery of their so-called marriage. Rosamond tries to escape to Paris, but Tempest pursues her. For two years, he follows Rosamond around Europe. She soon loathes the man she once thought she loved. Having experienced enough excitement, she returns chastened to her grandfather.

Such explicit stories were quite daring for the times. Single women weren't supposed to know about sexual desires, let alone have them. They reveal a passion in Louisa that remains quite hidden within the author of *Little Women*. During these years, Louisa also worked on *Hospital Sketches*, a brutal account of what she'd seen while working at the Union Army hospital.

Thanks to her writing, Louisa was now somewhat successful, and her family, including Bronson, expressed their delight. Undoubtedly, they were proud of her, and she was also the main support of her family. In 1863, she earned $600. Very little of that money went to Louisa. Instead, she paid household bills and sent her sister May on vacation.

The novel *Moods,* which Louisa has written years earlier, was finally published just before Christmas in 1864. She handed out copies as presents while Abigail clipped all the reviews. The reviews were mixed, and the book didn't sell very well. Lauded as a romance, the cold ending where the heroine rejects both suitors was not very popular.

Louisa had always wanted to see Europe. The family finances, however, would not allow for such a luxury. Finally, in 1865, she had an opportunity to travel as a companion with a young invalid woman named Anna. Louisa grasped at the chance. Her hospital experience made her a logical caretaker, but although she had spent most of her life taking care of others, Louisa often became impatient with Anna during the trip. In the end, she split from Anna and went to explore England and Paris on her own. She thoroughly enjoyed the remainder of the journey.

As soon as Louisa returned home to Concord, Abigail fired the housekeeper who had taken care of the family during Louisa's yearlong absence. Louisa returned to the same duties and worries that she'd happily left behind, and she was forced to pay the bills her family had incurred during her absence. Such was her welcome home after a free-spirited absence.

The good news was that her father, once so critical of her, now invited her to his discussion groups with notables such as Emerson, Margaret Fuller, and Nathaniel Hawthorne.

Chapter Seven

Little Women

"I am not afraid of storms, for I am learning how to sail my ship."

—Louisa May Alcott

Following her return from Europe, Louisa spent every day in her room at Orchard House working on her new children's book, *Little Women.* The book is highly autobiographical and contains the themes that had affected Louisa's family throughout her life. Louisa portrays herself as the headstrong Jo.

It was Louisa's publisher, Thomas Niles, who had initially asked her to write a children's book about girls. She didn't like the idea at first and wanted to put together a few of her lurid short stories for publication in a book. Louisa truly enjoyed writing about the racy darker side of life, but Niles kept pushing her, as did her father, to write a commercially profitable children's book instead. Finally, she agreed.

Louisa did not enjoy writing *Little Women.* Her meals mainly consisted of squash pies as she was giving most of her money to her mother. All she wanted to do was earn a good sum of money to help support her family. Even worse, Louisa's publisher considered the first few chapters she sent him dull and uninteresting. His young niece, however, loved them, and so did her little friends. Both Niles and Louisa were surprised at the response.

Little Women is about the lives of four sisters. They are modeled after Louisa and her own sisters and are named Meg, Jo, Beth, and Amy. The four girls move from childhood to adulthood in different ways with the help of their mother, Marmee. The family is impoverished, and the father is away preaching. As the novel opens, the mother and her daughters face Christmas on their own. It's a sad occasion for all.

The reader sees the girls grow up during a year. The two oldest daughters, Meg and Jo, teach in order to earn enough money for the family. Jo tries to write to earn more money and is quite successful at it. Their father returns home the following Christmas. Meg, the oldest girl, marries her love, John, and they plan a family of their own. Jo meanwhile goes to New York to work as a governess. She stays at a boarding house and begins to take German lessons from another lodger, Professor Bhaer. To earn more money with her writing, Jo writes stories that are popular but have no moral meaning (much like Louisa's lurid tales). Before Jo returns home, Professor Bhaer tells her she should improve her writing and not waste her time on sensationalism. When Bhaer comes to visit, he proposes to Jo, who finally agrees to marry him. Jo and Bhaer turn an old house into a boys' school.

There is nothing complicated about the plot of four girls struggling with adulthood and finding out what they really value. Louisa is telling the story of her family—with a few fantasies about how she wished it had been. The importance of family closeness serves as the major theme in *Little Women*. Regardless of how different they are, the sisters love and look out for each other. The narrator, through the character of Jo, struggles with becoming independent and supporting her entire family while being convinced that female submission is the secret to a happy home. It is an issue that Louisa struggled with her whole life.

Marmee, the mother, teaches the girls that their joy will come from having a devoted husband. The girls spend time finding appropriate husbands. In real life, Louisa never married. When her sisters did, Louisa saw it as a breaking of the sisterly bond they shared while growing up.

Little Women also touches on the theme of poverty. In the novel, Marmee teaches her girls that love is far more important than money. Considering Louisa's struggle, and occasional resentment, at having to support her family, this would be the author being good, the way women were expected to be good by nature. Louisa loved her family but considered having to support them a duty. Louisa's sisters, as do Jo's sisters, strongly believe in doing the right and moral thing. Duty is taken very seriously.

While Louisa had a father who did not always do his duty, she creates a father for the sisters who is a preacher with strong morals. Undoubtedly, the fictional father is the father she wished she'd had. Louisa's childhood was filled with tantrums, or, more precisely, an honest expression of angry feelings. The duality of being good and moral and being honest about her real emotions was difficult for her, mainly because her father refused to acknowledge those negative emotions.

Chapter Eight

Little Men

"It takes so little to make a child happy, that it is a pity in a world full of sunshine and pleasant things, that there should be any wistful faces, empty hands, or lonely little hearts."

—Louisa May Alcott

After the completion of *Little Women,* Louisa and her youngest sister May went on an extended trip throughout Europe, enjoying the sights. While they were traveling, Louisa became ill due to the mercury poisoning she'd been subjected to while working as a nurse but soon recovered.

When Louisa received a letter informing of Anna's husband's death, she began writing a sequel to *Little Woman* called *Little Men.* This was to assure that there would be enough money for Anna's children to be well taken care of financially. This Louisa still considered her responsibility. Leaving May in Europe to indulge in a flirtation, Louisa immediately headed back to Concord. She worked on her manuscript for *Little Men* every day.

Little Men, perhaps even more than *Little Women,* shows some of the ideological conflicts Louisa May had with feminism. In it, Jo and her husband, Bhaer, run a school for boys called Plumfield. While it was certainly unusual at the time for a woman to run a boys' school, the rebellious Jo takes on a motherly role regarding the boys. She takes on an expected feminine persona, and when some of the boys need special attention because of disabilities, she provides it.

One of the most interesting elements of the book is Jo and Bhaer's attempt to help Dan, a troubled student. Rare for its times, the school does not permit the hitting of students. Jo uses a lot of Bronson's educational techniques in her teaching—individuality must be respected, and learning should never be by rote but should bring enjoyment. Both Jo and Bhaer also insist that creative play is as critical to learning and character formation.

Louisa's attitude about feminism is played out in the only two female students of the school, Daisy and Nan. Daisy fits the traditional feminine mold, while Nan is the wild tomboy. As a writer, Louisa treats both characters as having equal virtues. She respects Daisy and at the same time encourages Nan to become a physician.

In between the publication of *Little Women* and *Little Men*, Louisa wrote a straight-forward morality story. Titled *An Old-Fashioned Girl*, it was the story of a country girl aged 14. Set in 1870, Polly Milton, the titular girl, visits a family in the big city. She is suitably impressed with their wealth, but she can't understand how these rich people can live without affection for each other and why they seem unhappy. While she stays with them, she deliberately remains in the background.

The family's daughter makes fun of Polly because of her simple dresses and country manners. Still, the family can't help but like this down-to-earth, old-fashioned girl. Polly visits the family regularly and is soon considered a part of the family. She eventually moves to the big city to give piano lessons. After a while, Polly finds out that this wealthy family is actually broke and in dire straits financially. At that point, Polly gently teaches them that family is more important than wealth. Slowly, the family changes and embraces a happier life. In the end, Polly ends up marrying the family's son, Tom.

An Old-Fashioned Girl seems like a strange story for Louisa to be writing, but in it, she imparts the same lessons as in *Little Women* in a simpler way. People make mistakes. They can grow and improve and change their behavior. As their behavior improves, so does their life. Money cannot buy happiness. While Polly is almost too perfect, it is the family that overcomes unhappiness by making personal changes to inspire growth that makes this an interesting tale. While the lessons in *An Old-Fashioned Girl* are simple, they are still relevant today.

Chapter Nine

Louisa May Alcott and Feminism

"I mean to vote before I die, even if my daughters have to carry me!"

—Abigail Alcott

Little Women is universally acclaimed as a feminist inspiration for young girls everywhere. Her characters are portrayed as fearlessly facing life's ordeals in a spirited way. The most spirited, of course, is Jo, who is based on Louisa herself.

Louisa was tasked at an early age with helping to support her family, which for the most part, she did without complaint. However, she had dreams beyond making a home and raising a family. She intended to be independent of anyone, even a husband. Yet reading *Little Women*, we see the four sisters dreaming of marriage and creating the ideal home when, in fact, Louisa hated the idea of marriage. Some have blamed Louisa for giving up her adventure stories for the more conventional morality books. Either way, Louisa's dreams of wealth and fame came true.

So, who was the real Louisa May Alcott? The woman who craved independence above all, or the writer who created a novel about the perfect family life, with all its sacrifices? Especially in the second part of *Little Women,* we witness the sisters becoming more conventional. Meg marries and creates her own family. Young Amy becomes involved with and marries the perennial boy-next-door. Even Jo weds, although an older man, and has two boys of her own. However, this is in effect an act of rebellion as she has previously turned down a proposal from Laurie, the boy-next-door who ends up marrying Amy. Jo makes it clear she has no intentions of becomes a proper wife. In the end, Jo marries Professor Bhaer, who is much older than she is and does not expect a typical mate.

Still, feminists since the mid-nineteenth century have discussed and argued about Jo's marriage. Was this an act of deliberate anti-feminism? Some accuse Louisa of betraying her ideals. Others have pointed out that true feminism lies in doing exactly what you want. Louisa and her doubleganger Jo always do what they want, even if it appears contradictory. They do not feel compelled to please anyone. In addition, Jo continues to write and teach, not the usual pursuits of married women of that era.

Neither Louisa nor Jo has any desire to become feminine. However, when their respective mothers become ill, they instantly turn into dutiful daughters and take care of everything in a motherly and most feminine fashion. Amy teases Jo about her life not turning out as adventuresome as she planned. Jo tells her, "Yes, I remember, but the life I wanted then seems selfish, lonely, and cold to me now. I haven't given up the hope that I may write a good book yet, but I can wait, and I'm sure it will be all the better for such experiences and illustrations as these."

Jo and Louisa are women who can accept themselves with whatever imperfections they may have. Some would consider that the very essence of feminism. Louisa was actually more rebellious than radical. She saw the problems that women had to endure but didn't necessarily want to change the world; she merely wanted to find comfort and be moral in her limited space in a male-run society.

The four sisters' mandate to be good and moral has been taught to them by their Marmee, who truly lives for her daughters. But how good was Marmee herself? She shocks Jo by confessing, "I've learned to check the hasty words that rise to my lips, and when I feel that they mean to break out against my will, I just go away for a minute, and give myself a little shake for being so weak and wicked." Mothers, and other moral people, have a duty to suppress their anger and leave it unexpressed. It was not a duty that Louisa appreciated.

The debate of how much of a feminist radical Louisa May Alcott actually was will undoubtedly continue. She lived a somewhat contradictory life that does not offer any easy answers.

Both of her parents, Abigail and Bronson, were political thinkers and abolitionists. Bronson, although a difficult man and father, spent his life advocating the rights of children and their education. He lost several teaching jobs because of his methods, including having the audacity to permit a black child into his schoolroom. Abigail was a suffragette who tried to expose her four daughters to as much freedom as possible, certainly more freedom than the average young girl in the mid-nineteenth century enjoyed.

This was when the highest virtue a girl could claim was to conform to societal norms.

Conclusion

The third and last book in the *Little Women* series was published in 1886. Entitled *Jo's Boys,* the book follows the lives of the Plumfield boys and Jo's two sons. By the time of its publication, Louisa had already been struggling with chronic health problems for years, most likely stemming from the mercury poisoning she'd been exposed to while nursing the wounded during the American Civil War. On March 6, 1888, two days after the death of her father, Louisa passed away at age 55 in Boston. She was buried close to her dear friends, Thoreau and Emerson, in the Sleepy Hollow Cemetery in Concord.

Louisa May Alcott was born into a time when women were not supposed to be noticed. Women knew their purpose, and that was to support their husbands and raise their children. Louisa's parents were radicals in their beliefs; they were abolitionists and encouraged their four daughters to excel. Still, excelling meant being good wives and mothers.

While her sisters followed that path, Louisa brushed aside any thought of marriage and frankly admitted she wanted fame and fortune. She assumed writing would get her what she wanted, and she was right. Her books, especially *Little Women,* sold well and enabled her to support her family. Feminists and suffragettes that came after her followed her lead in demanding independence from men. Still, Louisa May Alcott wanted more than not having to depend on a man—her desire for freedom extended to all, including slaves.

Made in the USA
Coppell, TX
30 June 2025

51304537R00024